W9-AOA-204

The PROMISE of SPRING

The PROMISE of SPRING

PHOTOGRAPHY BY
WILLIAM H. JOHNSON

Guideposts

NASHVILLE, TENNESSEE

ISBN 0-8249-5898-5

Published by Ideals Publications
535 Metroplex Drive, Suite 250
Nashville, Tennessee 37211
www.idealsbooks.com

Copyright © 2006 by Ideals Publications

All rights reserved. No part of this publication may be reproduced or transmitted in any form or by any means, electronic or mechanical, including photocopy, recording, or any information storage and retrieval system, without permission in writing from the publisher.

Printed and bound in the U.S.A. by RR Donnelley

Publisher and Editor, Patricia A. Pingry
Designer, Georgina Chidlow-Rucker
Copy Editor, Melinda Rathjen
Permissions Editor, Patsy Jay

10 9 8 7 6 5 4 3 2 1

ACKNOWLEDGMENTS

CROWELL, GRACE NOLL. "Hope" from *Poems of Inspiration and Courage* by Grace Noll Crowell. Copyright © 1928 and 1934 by Harper & Row, renewed 1956 and 1962 by the author. "Young Girl in Spring" and "Young Lincoln" from *Apples of Gold* by Grace Noll Crowell. Copyright 1950 by Harper & Bros. Used by permission of HarperCollins Publishers. DICKINSON, EMILY. "A Light Exists in Spring . . ." and "Constant" from *The Poems of Emily Dickinson*, edited by Ralph W. Franklin, Cambridge, Mass: The Belknap Press of Harvard University Press, Copyright © 1951–1998 by the President and Fellows of Harvard College. Reprinted by permission of the publishers and Trustees of Amherst College. GUITERMAN, ARTHUR. "Hills" from *General Putnam*. Copyright © 1935. Published by EP Dutton, an imprint of the Penguin Group (USA). JEFFERS, ROBINSON. "The Excesses of God" from *Angry At the Sun*. Copyright © 1941 by the author. Published by Random House. McFADDEN, ISOBEL. "April" from *Reward and Other Poems* by Isobel McFadden. Published by Ryerson Press. SEAMAN, HELLENE. "The Hills Keep Holy Ground" from *The Christian Century* and used by their permission. STIDGER, WILLIAM L. "I Saw God Wash the World" and "A Day." Used by permission of William S. Hyland. STITCH, WILHELMINA. "Blessed Are They" from *Silken Threads*. Copyright © 1930. Published by EPDutton, an imprint of The Penguin Group (USA). STRONG, PATIENCE. "Hope Is Like the Sun" and "The Unbroken String." Used by permission of Rupert Crew Ltd., London. Our sincere thanks to the following authors or their heirs, some of whom we were unable to locate: Clifton Abbott for "Just Keep On," Beverly J. Anderson for "Hope," Joseph Auslander for "A Blackbird Suddenly," John Gardiner Brainard for "I Saw Two Clouds At Morning," Esther York Burkholder for "Hope's Promise," Countee Cullen for "I Have a Rendezvous With Life," Eleanor Lyons Culver for "I Heard Him," Mary Carolyn Davies for "A Prayer for Every Day" and "Leading," Charles Divine for "We Met on Roads of Laughter," Max Eastman for "Rainy Song," Newman Flower for "A Creed in a Garden," Theodosia Garrison for "Shade," Strickland Gillilan for "Need of Loving," James Robert Gilmore for "Three Days," Sara Henderson Hay for "Prayer in April," Elma V. Harnetiaux for "Hope Is a Word to Live By," Orrick Johns for "Little Things," Mildred Keeling for "God's World," Florence Scripps Kellogg for "My Hand In God's," S. E. Kiser for "A Profitable Day," Minnie Klemme for "Hope for Tomorrow," Douglas Malloch for "Another Day," Angela Morgan for "God the Artist," Carrie May Nichols for "The Boomerang," John Jerome Rooney for "The Woodland Singer," R. L. Sharpe for "A Bag of Tools," Philip Sidney for "My True Love Hath My Heart," Anne Springsteen for "This Morning," Blanche Shoemaker Wagstaff for "All Paths Lead to You," and Emma Boge Whisenand for "Open Your Eyes."

Every effort has been made to establish ownership and use of each selection in this book. If contacted, the publisher will be pleased to rectify any inadvertent errors or omissions in subsequent editions.

CONTENTS

The Promise

of Spring

April Rain
Robert Loveman

It is not raining rain to me,
It's raining daffodils;
In every dimpled drop I see
Wildflowers on the hills.

The clouds of gray engulf the day
And overwhelm the town.
It is not raining rain to me;
It's raining roses down.

It is not raining rain to me,
But fields of clover bloom,
Where any buccaneering bee
May find a bed and room.

A health unto the happy!
A fig for him who frets!
It is not raining rain to me;
It's raining violets.

A Primrose by the Wayside
Anna Bunston de Bary

Close to the road's impurity,
It knows of nothing base,
So meekly and so trustfully
It lifts its lovely face.

So innocent, and yet with art
Incomparably sweet,
It leaned up and caressed my heart
While lying at my feet.

Can anything so fair and free
Be fashioned out of clay?
Then God may yet cull flowers from me
Some holy summer day.

Under a Wiltshire Apple Tree

Anna Bunston de Bary

Some folk as can afford,
So I've heard say,
Set up a sort of cross
Right in the garden way
To mind 'em of the Lord.

But I, when I do see
This apple tree
An' stoopin' limb
All spread wi' moss,
I think of Him
And how He talks wi' me.

I think of God
And how He trod
That garden long ago;
He walked, I reckon, to and fro
And then sat down
Upon the groun'
Or some low limb
What suited Him
Such as you see
On many a tree,
And on this very one
Where I at set o' sun

Do sit and talk wi' Him.
And, mornings too, I rise and come
An' sit down where the branch be low;
A bird do sing, a bee do hum,
The flowers in the border blow,
And all my heart's so glad and clear
As pools when mists do disappear:

As pools a-laughing in the light
When mornin' air is swep' an' bright,
As pools what got all heaven in sight
So's my heart's cheer
When He be near.
He never pushed the garden door,
He left no footmark on the floor;
I never heard Him stir nor tread
And yet His Hand do bless my head,
And when 'tis time for work to start
I takes Him with me in my heart.

And when I die, pray God I see
At very last this apple tree
An' stoopin' limb,
And think of Him
And all He's been to me.

A Prayer in Spring

Robert Frost

Oh, give us pleasure in the flowers today;
And give us not to think so far away
As the uncertain harvest; keep us here
All simply in the springing of the year.

Oh, give us pleasure in the orchard white,
Like nothing else by day, like ghosts by night;
And make us happy in the happy bees,
The swarm dilating round the perfect trees.

And make us happy in the darting bird
That suddenly above the bees is heard,
The meteor that thrusts in with needle bill,
And off a blossom in midair stands still.

For this is love and nothing else is love,
The which it is reserved for God above
To sanctify to what far ends He will,
But which it only needs that we fulfill.

GOD'S WORLD
EDNA ST. VINCENT MILLAY

O World, I cannot hold thee close enough!
    Thy winds, thy wide gray skies!
    Thy mists that roll and rise!
Thy woods, this autumn day, that ache and sag
And all but cry with color! That gaunt crag
To crush! To lift the lean of that black bluff!
World, World, I cannot get thee close enough!

Long have I known a glory in it all,
    But never knew I this;
    Here such a passion is
As stretcheth me apart. Lord, I do fear
Thou'st made the world too beautiful this year.
My soul is all but out of me—let fall
No burning leaf; prithee, let no bird call.

LEADING
MARY CAROLYN DAVIES

Forests are made for weary men,
That they may find their souls again,
And little leaves are hung on trees
To whisper of old memories.
And trails with cedar shadows black
Are placed there just to lead men back
Past all the pitfalls of success
To boyhood's faith and happiness.
Far from the city's craft and fraud,
O Forest, lead me back to God.

This is God's hospitality.

SHADE

THEODOSIA GARRISON

The kindliest thing God ever made,
His hand of very healing laid
Upon a fevered world, is shade.

His glorious company of trees
Throw out their mantles, and on these
The dust-stained wanderer finds ease.

Green temples, closed against the beat
Of noontime's blinding glare and heat,
Open to any pilgrim's feet.

The white road blisters in the sun;
Now half the weary journey done,
Enter and rest, O weary one!

And feel the dew of dawn still wet
Beneath thy feet, and so forget
The burning highway's ache and fret.

This is God's hospitality,
And whoso rests beneath a tree
Hath cause to thank Him gratefully.

DAISIES

BLISS CARMAN

Over the shoulders and slopes of the dune
I saw the white daisies go down to the sea,
A host in the sunshine, an army in June,
The people God sends us to set our hearts free.

The bobolinks rallied them up from the dell,
The orioles whistled them out of the wood;
And all of their singing was, "Earth, it is well!"
And all of their dancing was, "Life, thou art good!"

LITTLE THINGS

ORRICK JOHNS

There's nothing very beautiful and
　　nothing very gay
About the rush of faces in the
　　town by day;
But a light tan cow in a pale
　　green mead—
That is very beautiful, beautiful
　　indeed.
And the soft March wind and the
　　low March mist
Are better than kisses in a dark
　　street kissed.
The fragrance of the forest when
　　it wakes at dawn,
The fragrance of a trim green
　　village lawn,

The hearing of the murmur of the
　　rain at play—
These things are beautiful, beautiful
　　as day!
And I shan't stand waiting for love
　　or scorn
When the feast is laid for a day
　　new-born.
Oh, better let the little things I loved
　　when little
Return when the heart finds the great
　　things brittle;
And better is a temple made of bark
　　and thong
Than a tall stone temple that may
　　stand too long.

Bring summer and ripe fruits.

Pear Tree
Hilda Doolittle

Silver dust
lifted from the earth,
higher than my arms reach,
you have mounted.
O silver,
higher than my arms reach
you front us with great mass;
no flower ever opened

so staunch a white leaf,
no flower ever parted silver
from such rare silver;
O white pear,
your flower-tufts,
thick on the branch,
bring summer and ripe fruits
in their purple hearts.

Symbol
David Morton

My faith is all a doubtful thing,
Wove on a doubtful loom,
Until there comes, each
    showery spring,
A cherry tree in bloom;

And Christ, who died upon
    a tree
That death had stricken bare,
Comes beautifully back to me,
In blossoms everywhere.

SPINNING IN APRIL

JOSEPHINE PRESTON PEABODY

Moon in heaven's garden,
    among the clouds that wander,
Crescent moon so young to see,
    above the April ways,
Whiten, bloom not yet, not yet,
    within the twilight yonder;
All my spinning is not done,
    for all the loitering days.

Oh, my heart has two wild wings
    that ever would be flying!
Oh, my heart's a meadowlark that
    ever would be free!
Well it is that I must spin until
    the light is dying;
Well it is the little wheel must turn
    all day for me!

All the hilltops beckon, and beyond
    the western meadows
Something calls for ever, calls me
    ever, low and clear:
A little tree as young as I,
    the coming summer shadows—
The voice of running waters that I
    always thirst to hear.

Oftentimes the plea of it has set
    my wings a-beating;
Oftentimes it coaxes, as I sit
    weary-wise,
Till the wild life hastens out to
    wild things all entreating,
And leaves me at the spinning-wheel
    with dark, unseeing eyes.

A BLACKBIRD SUDDENLY

JOSEPH AUSLANDER

Heaven is in my hand, and I
Touch a heartbeat of the sky,
Hearing a blackbird's cry.

Strange, beautiful, unquiet thing,
Lone flute of God,
    how can you sing
Winter to spring?

You have outdistanced every
    voice and word,
And given my spirit wings
    until it stirred
Like you—a bird!

THE WOODLAND SINGER

JOHN JEROME ROONEY

There runs a rhythm thro' the woods and seas;
In the dark pines and from the wayside rose
A mystic soul of hidden motion blows,
A breath of life, a pulse within the breeze,
Weaving all discords to its harmonies;
And, as its wave alternate comes and goes,
A living power, a deathless essence flows
And moves all things and all things bounden frees.

Within this woodland lodge, remote, apart—
He heard spring's footfall on the circling hills,
The rain's soft whisper, the young violet's stir;
Yea, and he heard humanity's great heart
Throbbing afar amid its joys and ills,
And he their herald and interpreter!

A Creed in a Garden

Newman Flower

I believe in the God of my garden;
   the God of the trees,
The God with the feet of the fairy
   who treads on the breeze
And makes of the rose leaves a carpet;
   The God of the light,
The God of the dusk and the sunset;
   the God of the night
Who freshens the scents in my garden
   with breaths of the earth
And juggles and frets with the tulip
   and brings it to birth.
I believe in the God of the thorn-bud,
   the God of the bird
Who fashions a song from an eggshell;
   of the new world stirr'd
By the sudden comfort of April;
   the God of all grief
In the whimpering pain and the death
   of the leaf.
I believe in the God of the sky paths,
   whose cumbersome cloud
Shakes warm, laughing rain o'er my
   garden and whispers aloud
To the slumbering ant and the earthworm,
   to the uttermost weed
His challenge of Life and Achievement—
   That is my creed.

I believe in the God of the sky.

EVENTIDE

CAROLINE ATHERTON MASON

At cool of day, with God I walk
My garden's grateful shade;
I hear His voice among the trees,
And I am not afraid.

He speaks to me in every wind,
He smiles from every star;
He is not deaf to me, nor blind,
Nor absent, nor afar.

His hand that shuts the flowers to sleep,
Each in its dewy fold,
Is strong my feeble life to keep,
And competent to hold.

The powers below and powers above
Are subject to His care;
I cannot wander from His love
Who loves me everywhere.

Thus dowered, and guarded thus, with Him
I walk this peaceful shade;
I hear His voice among the trees,
And I am not afraid.

HYACINTHS TO FEED THY SOUL

GULISTAN OF MOSLIH EDDIN SAADI

If of thy mortal good thou art bereft,
And from thy slender store two loaves
    alone to thee are left,
Sell one, and with the dole
Buy hyacinths to feed thy soul.

OUT IN THE FIELDS WITH GOD
AUTHOR UNKNOWN

The little cares that fretted me,
I lost them yesterday,
Among the fields above the sea,
Among the winds at play,
Among the lowing of the herds,
The rustling of the trees,
Among the singing of the birds,
The humming of the bees.

The foolish fears of what might pass,
I cast them all away
Among the clover-scented grass
Among the new-mown hay,
Among the rustling of the corn
Where drowsy poppies nod,
Where ill thoughts die and good are born—
Out in the fields with God!

Buy hyacinths to feed thy soul.

In the Heart
Anna Bunston de Bary

O little lark, you need not fly
To seek your Master in the sky,
He treads our native sod;
Why should you sing aloft, apart?
Sing to the heaven of my heart;
In me, in me, in me is God!

O strangers passing in your car,
You pity me who come so far
On dusty feet, ill shod;
You cannot guess, you cannot know
Upon what wings of joy I go
Who travel home with God.

From far-off lands they bring your fare,
Earth's choicest morsels are your share,
And prize of gun and rod;
At richer boards I take my seat,
Have dainties angels may not eat:
In me, in me, in me is God!

O little lark, sing loud and long
To Him who gave you flight and song,
And me a heart aflame.
He loveth them of low degree,
And He hath magnified me,
And holy, holy, holy is His name!

A Strip of Blue
Lucy Larcom

I do not own an inch of land,
But all I see is mine,
The orchard and the mowing-fields,
The lawns and gardens fine.

The winds my tax collectors are,
They bring me tithes divine,
Wild scents and subtle essences,
A tribute rare and free;

And, more magnificent than all,
My window keeps for me
A glimpse of blue immensity,
A little strip of sea.

Here sit I, as a little child;
The threshold of God's door
Is that clear band of chrysoprase
Now the vast temple floor,

The blinding glory of the dome
I bow my head before.
Thy universe, O God, is home,
In height or depth, to me;

Yet here upon thy footstool green
Content am I to be;
Glad when is oped unto my need
Some sea-like glimpse of Thee.

O little lark, sing loud and long . . .

THE HILLS KEEP HOLY GROUND

HELLENE SEAMAN

When morning moves in slow processional
To worship day, the hills keep holy ground,
Where spirit meets in high confessional
The presence of Infinity, and sound
Of an eternal power stirs the air.
From silence unto silence echoes roll
The deep acclaim of consciousness aware
Of oneness with the universal soul.

No prophet blessed the quiet of these hills,
Nor stood at prayer before their solitude.
But in their boundless peace the mind fulfills
Diameters of vision that include
Eternity, the instant of God's hand—
Who worships here has found the Holy Land.

THE HILL-BORN

MAXWELL STRUTHERS BURT

You who are born of the hills,
Hill-bred, lover of hills,
Though the world may not treat you aright,
Though your soul be aweary with ills,
This will you know above other men:
In the hills you will find your peace again.

You who were nursed on the heights,
Hill-bred, lover of skies,
Though your love and your hope and your heart,
Though your trust be hurt till it dies,
This will you know above other men:
In the hills you will find your faith again.

You who are brave from the winds,
Hill-bred, lover of winds,
Though the God whom you know seems dim,
Seems lost in a mist that blinds,
This will you know above other men:
In the hills you will find your God again.

HILLS

ARTHUR GUITERMAN

I never loved your plains,
Your gentle valleys,
Your drowsy country lanes
And pleachèd alleys.

I want my hills—the trail
That scorns the hollow.
Up, up the ragged shale
Where few will follow.

Up, over wooded crest
And mossy boulder
With strong thigh, heaving chest,
And swinging shoulder,

So let me hold my way,
By nothing halted,
Until, at close of day
I stand exalted

High on my hills of dreams,
Dear hills that know me.
And then, how fair will seem
The lands below me,

How pure at vesper-time
The far bells chiming!
God, give me hills to climb
And strength for climbing!

God, give me hills to climb

THIS IS MY FATHER'S WORLD

MALTBIE D. BABCOCK

This is my Father's world,
And to my listening ears,
All nature sings, and round me rings
The music of the spheres.
This is my Father's world:
I rest me in the thought
Of rocks and trees, of skies and seas;
His hand the wonders wrought.

This is my Father's world;
The birds their carols raise;
The morning light, the lily white,
Declare their Maker's praise.
This is my Father's world:
He shines in all that's fair;
In the rustling grass I hear Him pass;
He speaks to me everywhere.

This is my Father's world,
Oh! let me ne'er forget
That though the wrong seems oft so strong,
God is the Ruler yet.
This is my Father's world:
The battle is not done;
Jesus who died shall be satisfied,
And earth and heaven be one.

THE GLORY OF GOD IN CREATION

THOMAS MOORE

Thou art, O God, the life and light
Of all this wondrous world we see;
Its glow by day, its smile by night,
Are but reflections caught from Thee.
Where'er we turn, Thy glories shine,
And all things fair and bright are Thine!

When day, with farewell beam, delays
Among the opening clouds of even,
And we can almost think we gaze
Through golden vistas into heaven—
Those hues that make the sun's decline
So soft, so radiant, Lord! are Thine.

When night, with wings of starry gloom,
O'ershadows all the earth and skies,
Like some dark, beauteous bird, whose plume
Is sparkling with unnumber'd eyes—
That sacred gloom, those fires divine,
So grand, so countless, Lord! are Thine.

When youthful Spring around us breathes,
Thy Spirit warms her fragrant sigh;
And every flower the Summer wreathes
Is born beneath Thy kindling eye:
Where'er we turn, Thy glories shine,
And all things fair and bright are Thine!

*All things
fair and bright
are Thine.*

God of the Earth, the Sky, the Sea

Samuel Longfellow

God of the earth, the sky, the sea,
Maker of all above, below,
Creation lives and moves in Thee;
Thy present life through all doth flow.

Thy love is in the sunshine's glow,
Thy life is in the quickening air;
When lightnings flash and storm winds blow,
There is Thy power, Thy law is there.

We feel Thy calm at evening's hour,
Thy grandeur in the march of night,
And when the morning breaks in power,
We hear Thy word, "Let there be light."

But higher far, and far more clear,
Thee in man's spirit we behold,
Thine image and Thyself are there,
Th' indwelling God, proclaimed of old.

MIRACLES

WALT WHITMAN

I believe a leaf of grass is no less than the journey-work of the stars,
And the pismire is equally perfect, and a grain of sand, and the egg of the wren,
And the tree-toad is a chef-d'oeuvre for the highest,
And the running blackberry would adorn the parlors of heaven,
And the narrowest hinge in my hand puts to scorn all machinery,
And the cow crunching with depress'd head surpasses any statue,
And a mouse is miracle enough to stagger sextillions of infidels.

EARTH'S COMMON THINGS

Minot J. Savage

Seek not afar for beauty. Lo! it glows
In dew-wet grasses all about thy feet;
In birds, in sunshine, childish faces sweet,
In stars and mountain summits topped
    with snows.

Go not abroad for happiness. For see,
It is a flower that blooms at thy door.
Bring love and justice home, and
    then no more
Thou'lt wonder in what dwelling
    joy may be.

Dream not of noble service
    elsewhere wrought;
The simple duty that awaits thy hand
Is God's voice uttering a divine command,
Life's common deeds build all that
    saints have thought.

In wonder-workings, or some bush aflame,
Met look for God and fancy Him concealed;
But in earth's common things He
    stands revealed
While grass and flowers and stars spell
    out His name.

Earth's crammed with heaven.

GLORY IN THE COMMONPLACE
ELIZABETH BARRETT BROWNING

Earth's crammed with heaven,
And every common bush afire with God;
But only he who sees, takes off his shoes;
The rest sit round it and pluck blackberries,
And daub their natural faces unaware
More and more from the first similitude.

I SAW GOD WASH THE WORLD
WILLIAM L. STIDGER

I saw God wash the world last night
With His sweet showers on high,
And then, when morning came, I saw
Him hang it out to dry.

He washed each tiny blade of grass
And every trembling tree;
He flung His showers against the hill,
And swept the billowing sea.

The white rose is a cleaner white,
The red rose is more red,
Since God washed every fragrant face
And put them all to bed.

There's not a bird, there's not a bee
That wings along the way
But is a cleaner bird and bee
Than it was yesterday.

I saw God wash the world last night.
Ah, would He had washed me
As clean of all my dust and dirt
As that old white birch tree.

THE EXCESSES OF GOD

Robinson Jeffers

Is it not by His high superfluousness we know
Our God? For to equal a need
Is natural, animal, mineral; but to fling
Rainbows over the rain
And beauty above the moon, and secret rainbows
On the domes of deep seashells,
And make the necessary embrace of breeding
Beautiful also as fire,
Not even the weeds to multiply without blossom
Nor the birds without music:
There is the great humaneness at the heart of things,
The extravagant kindness, the fountain
Humanity can understand, and would flow likewise
If power and desire were perch-mates.

APRIL

Isobel McFadden

Always the month of April fills
All of our world with colored thrills
Leaves on a tree on a low green hill
And crocus blooms where the sun lies still.
Always with eager hands she spills
Poems of gold on the daffodils,
And back of the miracles we see
Is the caring of God for you and me.

Even the rain in April sings,
Even the blue in a pair of wings,
And oh, the beauty of song that's heard
In the magical singing of a bird.
Even the bell in a snowdrop rings
Of tiny dreams of lovely things.
Even the chords in a weary heart
Sing with the wonder flowers impart!

A Light upon the Mountains

Henry Burton

There's a light upon the mountains,
And the day is at the spring,
When our eyes shall see the beauty
And the glory of the King:
Weary was our heart with waiting,
And the night-watch seemed so long,
But His triumph-day is breaking,
And we hail it with a song.

In the fading of the starlight
We may see the coming morn;
And the lights of men are paling
In the splendors of the dawn;
For the eastern skies are glowing
As with light of hidden fire,
And the hearts of men are stirring
With the throbs of deep desire.

There's a hush of expectation
And a quiet in the air,
And the breath of God is moving
In the fervent breath of prayer;
For the suffering, dying Jesus
Is the Christ upon the throne,
And the travail of our spirit
Is the travail of His own.

Hark! we hear a distant music,
And it comes with fuller swell;
'Tis the triumph-song of Jesus,
Of our King Immanuel!
Go ye forth with joy to meet Him!
And, my soul, be swift to bring
All thy sweetest and thy dearest
For the triumph of our King.'

PRAYER IN APRIL

Sara Henderson Hay

God grant that I may never be
A scoffer at Eternity—
As long as every April brings
The sweet rebirth of growing things;
As long as grass is green anew,
I shall believe that God looks down
Upon His wide earth, cold and brown,
To bless its unborn mystery
Of leaf, and bud, and flower to be;
To smile on it from tender skies—
How could I think it otherwise?
Had I been dust for many a year,
I still would know when spring was near,
For the good earth that pillowed me
Would whisper immortality,
And I, in part, would rise and sing
Amid the grasses murmuring.
When looking on the mother sod,
Can I doubt that this be God?
Or when a primrose smiles at me,
Can I distrust Eternity?

There's a light upon the mountains.

A Light Exists in Spring

Emily Dickinson

A light exists in spring
  Not present on the year
At any other period.
  When March is scarcely here

A color stands abroad
  On solitary hills
That silence cannot overtake,
  But human nature feels.

It waits upon the lawn;
  It shows the furthest tree
Upon the furthest slope we know;
  It almost speaks to me.

Then, as horizons step,
  Or noons report away,
Without the formula of sound,
  It passes, and we stay:

A quality of loss
  Affecting our content,
As trade had suddenly encroached
  Upon a sacrament.

I Heard Him

Eleanor Lyons Culver

I heard the great Creator's voice
    speak softly in the breeze.
I heard Him when He rustled all
    the branches in the trees.
I heard Him in the patter of a cool,
    refreshing shower,
And in the mighty river's boom I
    heard Him speak with power.
I heard Him in the chatter of a
    squirrel all dressed in fur,
And in the sweet contentment of
    a fuzzy kitten's purr.
I heard Him in the cricket's chirp
    one starry, summer night,
And when the saucy rooster crowed
    announcing morning's light.
I heard Him in a waterfall and in a
    singing creek,
And in the whisper of the pines,
    I'm sure I heard Him speak.
I felt the great Creator near in all
    His wondrous ways
And then I paused to bow my head
    in gratitude and praise.

A light exists in spring . . .

The Promise

of Morning

THE DAWN
AUTHOR UNKNOWN

One morn I rose and looked upon the world.
"Have I been blind until this hour?" I said.
On every trembling leaf the sun had spread,
And was like golden tapestry unfurled;
And as the moments passed, more light was hurled
Upon the drinking earth athirst for light;
And I, beholding all this wondrous sight,
Cried out aloud, "O God, I love Thy world!"
And since that waking, often I drink deep
The joy of dawn, and peace abides with me;
And though I know that I again shall see
Dark fear with withered hand approach my sleep,
More sure am I when lonely night shall flee,
At dawn the sun will bring good cheer to me.

OPEN YOUR EYES

EMMA BOGE WHISENAND

Open your eyes that you may see
The beauty that around you lies,
The misty loveliness of the dawn,
The glowing colors of the skies;
The child's bright eager eyes of blue,
The gnarled and wrinkled face of age,
The bird with crimson on his wing
Whose spirit never knew a cage;

The roadsides' blooming goldenrod
So brave through summer's wind and heat,
The brook that rushes to the sea
With courage that naught may defeat.
Open your eyes that you may see
The wonder that around you lies;
It will enrich your every day
And make you glad and kind and wise.

GOD'S GRANDEUR
GERARD MANLEY HOPKINS

The world is charged with the
　　grandeur of God.
It will flame out, like shining
　　from shook foil,
And for all this, nature is
　　never spent;
There lives the dearest freshness
　　deep down things;
And though the last lights from
　　the black west went,
Oh, morning at the brown brink
　　eastwards springs—
Because the Holy Ghost over
　　the bent
World broods with warm breast,
　　and with, ah, bright wings.

*The world
is charged
with the
grandeur
of God.*

TODAY
AUTHOR UNKNOWN

With every rising of the sun
Think of your life as just begun.

The past has cancelled and buried deep
All yesterdays. There let them sleep.

Concern yourself with but today.
Grasp it, and teach it to obey

Your will and plan. Since time began
Today has been the friend of man.

You and today! A soul sublime
And the great heritage of time.

With God himself to bind the twain,
Go forth, brave heart. Attain. Attain.

ANOTHER DAY
Douglas Malloch

Another dawn, another day,
Another chance another way—
To finish something you began,
Or else to try another plan.

Another sky, another sun,
Another and a better one,
Another day you never had,
Another reason to be glad.

Another day, another start,
A firmer hold, a braver heart,
A stronger arm, a wiser mind,
A mortal of another kind.

Another dawn, another day,
Another chance another way
To take a task and see it through—
Another world, another you!

WATCH THE CORNERS

Lulu Linton

When you wake up in the morning
    of a chill and cheerless day,
And feel inclined to grumble,
    pout or frown,
Just glance into your mirror
    and you will quickly see
It's just because the corners
    of your mouth turn down.
        Then take this simple rhyme,
        Remember it in time:
It's always dreary weather,
    in countryside or town,
When you wake and find the corners
    of your mouth turned down.

If you wake up in the morning
    full of bright and happy thoughts,
And begin to count the blessings
    in your cup,
Then glance into your mirror
    and you will quickly see
It's all because the corners
    of your mouth turn up.
        Then take this little rhyme,
        Remember all the time:
There's joy aplenty in this world
    to fill life's silver cup
If you'll only keep the corners
    of your mouth turned up.

THE OPTIMIST

JOSEPH B. STRAUSS

I love the play
Of every day,
And all the life force that we see;
To build anew,
To carry through,
And just to live is joy to me.

Though grief and ill
My hours may fill,
I shall not say all life is vain;

In spite of woe,
And blow on blow,
I shall not think there's naught but pain.

A touch of spring,
A bird on wing,
And now and then a warming smile;
A friend or two
With trust in you—
These, free to all, make life worthwhile.

Just to live is joy to me.

THE SALUTATION OF DAWN
FROM THE SANSKRIT

Listen to the Exhortation of the Dawn!
Look to this Day!
For it is Life, the very Life of Life.
In its brief course lie all the
Verities and Realities of your Existence;
    The Bliss of Growth,
    The Glory of Action,
    The Splendor of Beauty;
For Yesterday is but a Dream,
And Tomorrow is only a Vision;
But Today well lived makes every
Yesterday a Dream of Happiness, and every
Tomorrow a Vision of Hope.
Look well therefore to this Day!
Such is the Salutation of the Dawn.

WHEN THINGS GO WRONG
CHARLES HENRY CHESLEY

I count it best, when things go wrong,
To hum a tune and sing a song;
A heavy heart means sure defeat,
But joy is victory replete.

If skies are cloudy, count the gain,
New life depends upon the rain;
The cuckoo carols loud and long
When clouds hang low and things go wrong.

When things go wrong, remember then
The happy heart has strength of ten;
Forget the sorrow, sing a song—
It makes all right when things seem wrong.

THREE DAYS

JAMES ROBERT GILMORE

So much to do: so little done!
Ah! yesternight I saw the sun
Sink beamless down the vaulted gray,
The ghastly ghost of Yesterday.

So little done: so much to do!
Each morning breaks on conflicts new;

But eager, brave, I'll join the fray,
And fight the battle of Today.

So much to do: so little done!
But when it's o'er, the victory won,
Oh! then, my soul, this strife and sorrow
Will end in that great, glad Tomorrow.

A Receipt for Happiness

John Kendrick Bangs

Begin the day with smiling eyes;
Pursue the day with smiling lips;
Through clouds perceive the smiling skies,
Up where the smiling sunbeam trips.

Let smiling thoughts within your mind
Drive gloom and cold despair apart,

And promptings of a genial kind
Keep ever growing in your heart.

Meet trouble with a cheery mien,
Be jovial in the face of care—
He routs all mischief from the scene
Who greets it with a jocund air.

A Profitable Day

S. E. Kiser

Yesterday was not so good to me:
Things I had hoped to do were left undone;
The world was drab, or so it seemed to be;
Among the bruised and beaten I was one.
In many anterooms I cooled my heels,
While others won the favors that I sought;
If men whose luck was good enjoyed their meals,
No pearls were in the oysters that I got.

I had no cordial greeting anywhere,
As yesterday I made my weary round;
I hunted hard for prospects that were fair,
And blundered always on forbidden ground.
Suspicion seemed to be in every glance
That men whose time was precious cast my way;
I looked in vain for any lucky chance
And any sign of promise—yesterday.

But yesterday was not a total loss;
There was some useful practice that I had
In standing bravely up beneath my cross
And fighting through conditions that were bad.
I learned, I think, to be a little more
Adept in keeping back unbidden sighs;
My sympathy is deeper than before
For beaten men with dimmed and weary eyes.

And now it is today again—TODAY,
With chances that are still untried and new!
I may not find an unobstructed way
In which to seek the fortunes I pursue;
But yesterday is gone, and I can start
Today without regret and unashamed;
I have not let rebuffs crowd from my heart
The courage I have struggled for—and claimed.

MY PURPOSE
THOMAS DEKKER

To awaken each morning with a smile
    brightening my face;
To greet the day with reverence for the
    opportunities it contains;
To approach my work with a clean mind;
To hold ever before me, even in the doing
    of little things, the Ultimate Purpose
    toward which I am working;
To meet men and women with laughter
    on my lips and love in my heart;
To be gentle, kind, and courteous through
    all the hours;
To approach the night with weariness that
    ever woos sleep, and the joy that comes
    from work well done—
This is how I desire to waste wisely my days.

SONG
ROBERT BROWNING

The year's at the spring
And day's at the morn;
Morning's at seven:
The hillside's dew-pearled;
The lark's on the wing;
The snail's on the thorn;
God's in His heaven—
All's right with the world!

All's right with the world.

STILL, STILL WITH THEE

HARRIET BEECHER STOWE

Still, still with Thee, when purple morning breaketh,
When the bird waketh and the shadows flee;
Fairer than morning, lovelier than the daylight,
Dawns the sweet consciousness, I am with Thee!

Alone with Thee, amid the mystic shadows,
The solemn hush of nature newly born;
Alone with Thee, in breathless adoration,
In the calm dew and freshness of the morn.

Still, still with Thee, as to each newborn morning
A fresh and solemn splendor still is given,
So doth this blessed consciousness awakening,
Breathe, each day, nearness unto Thee and heaven.

When sinks the soul, subdued by toil, to slumber,
Its closing eye looks up to Thee in prayer;
Sweet the repose beneath Thy wings o'ershading,
But sweeter still to wake and find Thee there.

So shall it be at last, in that bright morning
When the soul waketh and life's shadows flee;
Oh, in that hour fairer than daylight dawning,
Shall rise the glorious thought, I am with Thee!

MORNING PRAYER

AUTHOR UNKNOWN

When little things would irk me, and I grow
Impatient with my dear ones, make me know
How in a moment joy can take its flight
And happiness be quenched in endless night.
Keep this thought with me all the livelong day
That I may guard the harsh words I might say
When I would fret and grumble, fiery hot,
At trifles that tomorrow are forgot—
Let me remember, Lord, how it would be
If these, my loved ones, were not here with me.

I Saw Two Clouds at Morning

John Gardiner Brainard

I saw two clouds at morning,
Tinged with the rising sun,
And in the dawn they floated on,
And mingled into one:
I thought that morning cloud was blest,
It moved so sweetly to the west.

I saw two summer currents
Flow smoothly to their meeting,
And join their course, with silent force,

In peace each other greeting:
Calm was their course through banks of green,
While dimpling eddies played between.

Such be your gentle motion,
Till life's last pulse shall beat;
Like summer's beam, and summer's stream,
Float on, in joy, to meet
A calmer sea, where storms shall cease—
A purer sky, where all is peace.

The word for me is joy . . .

TODAY

JOHN KENDRICK BANGS

Today, whatever may annoy,
The word for me is *joy*, just simple joy:
The joy of life;
The joy of children and of wife;
The joy of bright blue skies;
The joy of rain; the glad surprise
Of twinkling stars that shine at night;
The joy of winged things upon their flight;
The joy of noonday, and the tried
True joyousness of eventide;

The joy of labor, and of mirth;
The joy of air, and sea, and earth—
The countless joys that ever flow from Him
Whose vast beneficence doth dim
The lustrous light of day,
And lavish gifts divine upon our way.
  Whate'er there be of sorrow
  I'll put off till tomorrow,
And when tomorrow comes, why then
'Twill be today and joy again!

A Morning Prayer

Ella Wheeler Wilcox

Let me today do something that will take
A little sadness from the world's vast store,
And may I be so favored as to make
Of joy's too scanty sum a little more.

Let me not hurt, by any selfish deed
Or thoughtless word, the heart of foe or friend.
Nor would I pass unseeing worthy need,
Or sin by silence when I should defend.

However meager be my worldly wealth,
Let me give something that shall aid my kind—
A word of courage, or a thought of health
Dropped as I pass for troubled hearts to find.

Let me tonight look back across the span
'Twixt dawn and dark, and to my conscience say—
Because of some good act to beast or man—
"The world is better that I lived today."

Faith for Tomorrow

Thomas Curtis Clark

"Tomorrow, friend, will be another day,"
A seer wise of old was wont to say
To him who came at eventide, in grief,
Because the day had borne no fruitful sheaf.

O Lord of Life, that each of us might learn
From vain todays and yesterdays to turn,
To face the future with a hope newborn
That what we hope for cometh with the morn!

A Day

WILLIAM L. STIDGER

What does it take to make a day?
A lot of love along the way:
It takes a morning and a noon,
A father's voice, a mother's croon;
It takes some task to challenge all
The powers that a man may call
His own: the powers of mind and limb;
A whispered word of love; a hymn
Of hope—a comrade's cheer—
A baby's laughter and a tear;
It takes a dream, a hope, a cry
Of need from some soul passing by;
A sense of brotherhood and love;
A purpose sent from God above;
It takes a sunset in the sky,
The stars of night, the winds that sigh;
It takes a breath of scented air,
A mother's kiss, a baby's prayer.
That is what it takes to make a day:
A lot of love along the way.

*It takes
a dream,
a hope, a cry . . .*

THE BOOMERANG

Carrie May Nichols

One unkind word in the early morn
Will poison the thoughts for the day;
One unkind look to one we love
Will take all the sunshine away.
And twice all the sunshine we take away
From the lives of others at early day
We steal from ourselves the whole day long,
And we lose the beauty of earth's glad song.

One little smile when things go wrong
Will drive off many a frown;
One pleasant look, though the thoughts do rage,
Will put the tempter down.
And twice all the pleasure that we give out,
At the time when we are most tempted to pout,
Will sweeten our lives like a breath of May,
And the sun will shine through the whole glad day.

*And the sun
will shine
through the
whole glad
day.*

A Prayer for Every Day

Mary Carolyn Davies

Make me too brave to lie or be unkind.
Make me too understanding, too, to mind
The little hurts companions give, and friends,
The careless hurts that no one quite intends.
Make me too thoughtful to hurt others so.
Help me to know
The inmost hearts of those for whom I care,
Their secret wishes, all the loads they bear,
That I may add my courage to their own.
May I make lonely folks feel less alone,
And happy ones a little happier yet.
May I forget
What ought to be forgotten and recall,
Unfailing, all
That ought to be recalled,
    each kindly thing,
Forgetting what might sting.
To all upon my way,
Day after day,
Let me be joy, be hope! Let my life sing!

THIS MORNING

ANNE SPRINGSTEEN

Life has begun again, Father.
You have given me another day of grace,
Another day to live;
    to speak to someone,
    to touch someone,
    to ask for something,

    to take something,
    to give something.

Whatever I make of this day,
Whatever I become this day
I put into Your hands.

I Have a Rendezvous with Life
Countee Cullen

I have a rendezvous with Life,
In days I hope will come,
Ere youth has sped, and strength of mind,
Ere voices sweet grow dumb.
I have a rendezvous with Life,
When spring's first heralds hum.
Sure some would cry it's better far
To crown their days with sleep
Than face the road, the wind and rain,
To heed the calling deep.
Though wet nor blow nor space I fear,
Yet fear I deeply, too,
Lest Death should meet and claim me ere
I keep Life's rendezvous.

Today
Lydia Avery Coonley Ward

Why fear tomorrow, timid heart?
Why tread the future's way?
We only need to do our part
Today, dear child, today.

The past is written! Close the book
On pages sad and gay;
Within the future do not look,
But live today—today.

'Tis this one hour that God has given;
His Now we must obey;
And it will make our earth His heaven
To live today—today.

GOD'S WORLD
MILDRED KEELING

I'm glad I am living this morning
Because the day is so fair,
And I feel God's presence so keenly
About me everywhere.

The heavens declare His glory.
The trees seem to speak of His power;
And I see His matchless beauty
In each small, growing flower.

The rocks all tell of His wonder.
In the hills His strength I see;
And the birds are singing His praises
In the songs that they sing to me.

I read in the daylight His greatness,
And the night speaks again of His power;
The raindrops talk of His kindness
In each refreshing shower.

Oh, I'm glad to be living this morning
In a world of beauty so rare
Where the God of heaven is hovering
About me everywhere.

BEGIN AGAIN
SUSAN COOLIDGE

Every day is a fresh beginning,
Every morn is the world made new.
You who are weary of sorrow and sinning,
Here is a beautiful hope for you—
A hope for me and a hope for you.

Every day is a fresh beginning;
Listen, my soul, to the glad refrain,
And, spite of old sorrow and older sinning,
And puzzles forecasted and possible pain,
Take heart with the day, and begin again.

The Promise

of Youth

If

RUDYARD KIPLING

If you can keep your head when all about you
Are losing theirs and blaming it on you;
If you can trust yourself when all men doubt you,
But make allowance for their doubting too;
If you can wait and not be tired by waiting,
Or being lied about, don't deal in lies,
Or being hated, don't give way to hating,
And yet don't look too good, nor talk too wise;

If you can dream—and not make dreams your master;
If you can think—and not make thoughts your aim;
If you can meet with Triumph and Disaster
And treat those two impostors just the same;
If you can bear to hear the truth you've spoken
Twisted by knaves to make a trap for fools,
Or watch the things you gave your life to, broken,
And stoop and build 'em up with worn-out tools;

If you can make one heap of all your winnings
And risk it on one turn of pitch-and-toss,
And lose, and start again at your beginnings
And never breathe a word about your loss;
If you can force your heart and nerve and sinew
To serve your turn long after they are gone,
And so hold on when there is nothing in you
Except the Will which says to them: "Hold on!"

If you can talk with crowds and keep your virtue,
Or walk with Kings—nor lose the common touch;
If neither foes nor loving friends can hurt you;
If all men count with you, but none too much;
If you can fill the unforgiving minute
With sixty seconds' worth of distance run—
Yours is the Earth and everything that's in it,
And—which is more—you'll be a Man, my son!

I Remember, I Remember

Thomas Hood

I remember, I remember
The house where I was born,
The little window where the sun
Came peeping in at morn;
He never came a wink too soon
Nor brought too long a day;
But now, I often wish the night
Had borne my breath away.

I remember, I remember
The roses, red and white,
The violets, and the lily-cups—
Those flowers made of light!
The lilacs where the robin built,
And where my brother set
The laburnum on his birthday—
The tree is living yet!

I remember, I remember
Where I was used to swing,
And thought the air must rush as fresh
To swallows on the wing;
My spirit flew in feathers then
That is so heavy now,
And summer pools could hardly cool
The fever on my brow.

I remember, I remember
The fir trees dark and high;
I used to think their slender tops
Were close against the sky:
It was a childish ignorance,
But now 'tis little joy
To know I'm farther off from heaven
Than when I was a boy.

The Flight of Youth

Richard Henry Stoddard

There are gains for all our losses.
There are balms for all our pain:
But when youth, the dream, departs,
It takes something from our hearts,
And it never comes again.

We are stronger, and are better,
Under manhood's sterner reign:
Still we feel that something sweet
Followed youth, with flying feet,
And will never come again.

Something beautiful is vanished,
And we sigh for it in vain;
We behold it everywhere,
On the earth, and in the air,
But it never comes again!

As I Grow Old

Author Unknown

God keep my heart attuned
    to laughter
When youth is done;
When all the days are gray days,
    coming after
The warmth, the sun.
God keep me then from bitterness,
    from grieving,
When life seems cold;
God keep me always loving
    and believing
As I grow old.

God keep me always . . .

Young and Old

Charles Kingsley

When all the world is young, lad,
And all the trees are green;
And every goose a swan, lad,
And every lass a queen;
Then hey for boot and horse, lad,
And round the world away;
Young blood must have its course, lad,
And every dog his day.

When all the world is old, lad,
And all the trees are brown;
And all the sport is stale, lad,
And all the wheels run down:
Creep home, and take your place there,
The spent and maimed among;
God grant you find one face there
You loved when all was young.

Ode on Intimations of Immortality

William Wordsworth

Our birth is but a sleep and a forgetting:
The Soul that rises with us, our life's Star,
Hath had elsewhere its setting,
And cometh from afar:
Not in entire forgetfulness,
And not in utter nakedness,
But trailing clouds of glory do we come
From God, who is our home:
Heaven lies about us in our infancy!

All the trees are green . . .

PICKING BERRIES

MARGARET E. SANGSTER

Away to the hillside on swift little feet,
Trot quick through the meadows, in
 shadow and sun,
Broad brims and deep crowns over brows
 that are sweet,
And round rosy cheeks that are
 dimpling with fun.

And home from the hillside on slow little feet,
With baskets as heavy as faces are bright;
And who will be first the dear mother to greet,
And see her surprise and her look of delight?

But she never will dream, by the berries
 they bring,
Of the millions they left where the sweet
 berries grow,
Away on the hills where the merry birds sing,
And the brook dances down to the valley below.

PLAYTIME

WILLIAM BLAKE

When the voices of children are heard
 on the green
And laughing is heard on the hill,
My heart is at rest within my breast,
And everything else is still.

"Then come home, my children, the sun
 is gone down,
And the dews of night arise;
Come, come, leave off play, and let us away
Till the morning appears in the skies."

"No, no, let us play, for it is yet day,
And we cannot go to sleep;
Besides, in the sky the little birds fly,
And the hills are covered with sheep."

YOUNG GIRL IN SPRING

GRACE NOLL CROWELL

My calico dress was a silvery sheath,
My sturdy shoes were as light as a feather,
When I went out through the dappled woods,
A little girl in the glad May weather.
My basket of reeds was a thing of gold
With a glittering handle to swing and hold.

I was wild with joy at the first bluebell,
A-thrill with delight at a wild flower's capture,
While the sudden glimpse of a trillium bloom
Would stir my heart to exquisite rapture.
But oh, the heights of ecstasy when
I discovered the first wild cyclamen!

It was like a star that was shot from the sky
To fall at my feet like a radiant rocket.
I gathered it there—I gathered them all,
I filled my basket, my hat, my pocket:
A small happy vandal who did not know
That wild lovely things should be left
    where they grow.

MY HEART LEAPS UP

WILLIAM WORDSWORTH

My heart leaps up when I behold
    A rainbow in the sky;
So was it when my life began;
So is it now I am a man;
So be it when I shall grow old,
    Or let me die!
The Child is father of the Man;
And I could wish my days to be
Bound each to each by natural piety.

YOUTH

SAMUEL ULLMAN

Youth is not a time of life; it is a state
    of mind.
It is not a matter of rosy cheeks, red lips,
    and supple knees;
It is a matter of the will, a quality of
    the imagination,
A vigor of the emotions; it is the freshness
    of the deep springs of life.

GROW OLD ALONG WITH ME

ROBERT BROWNING

Grow old along with me!
The best is yet to be,
The last of life, for which the first
    was made.
Our times are in his hand
Who saith: "A whole I planned,
Youth shows but half; trust God,
    see all, nor be afraid."

CHEERFULNESS

AUTHOR UNKNOWN

I'm glad the sky is painted blue,
And the earth is painted green,
And such a lot of nice fresh air
All sandwiched in between.

The best is yet to be...

THE CHILD'S WORLD
WILLIAM BRIGHTY RANDS

Great, wide, beautiful, wonderful World,
With the wonderful water round you curled,
And the wonderful grass upon your breast,
World, you are beautifully dressed.

The wonderful air is over me,
And the wonderful wind is shaking the tree—
It walks on the water, and whirls in the mills,
And talks to itself on the top of the hills.

You friendly Earth, how far do you go,
With the wheat-fields that nod and the
        rivers that flow,
With cities and gardens and cliffs and isles,
And the people upon you for thousands
        of miles?

Ah! you are so great, and I am so small,
I hardly can think of you, World, at all;
And yet, when I said my prayers today,
My mother kissed me, and said, quite gay,

"If the wonderful World is great to you,
And great to father and mother too,
You are more than the Earth, though you are
        such a dot!
You can love and think, and the Earth cannot!"

HAPPY THOUGHT
ROBERT LOUIS STEVENSON

The world is so full of a number
        of things,
I'm sure we should all be as
        happy as kings.

AT EASTER

MARGARET E. SANGSTER

I did not grow tired of winter,
    I was glad of the snow and the cold;
I liked the weather when flake and feather
    Were flying o'er field and wold;
But now I am glad of the sunshine
    That is calling the robins back,
Of the beautiful flowers, the long bright hours,
    And the bloom in the springtime's track.

I am making a splendid garden
    With the plants that I love best;
There sparrows will quarrel o'er mint and laurel,
    And orioles hang a nest.
I shall bring from the deep old forest
    All fairylike things I see,
And trooping after, with song and laughter,
    The fairies will follow me.

I have heard that Mother Nature,
    A dame so wise and kind,
Is always spinning a sweet beginning
    For the lives she keeps in mind.
She tends the snowdrop hardy,
    And the jonquil's merry race,
She lines her pillows with pussy willows,
    And kisses the pansy's face.

You see, I am just eleven;
    I have lots of things to do;
And all of our learning is well worth earning,
    If what folks tell be true.
I am glad, so glad, 'tis Easter,
    When the tiny bluebells chime;
But, somehow, eleven is so near heaven,
    I am happy 'most all the time.

The Promise

of Love

Rainy Song
Max Eastman

Down the dripping pathway,
    dancing through the rain,
Brown eyes of beauty,
    laugh to me again!

Eyes full of starlight,
    moist over fire,
Full of young wonder,
    touch my desire!

Oh, like a brown bird,
    like a bird's flight,
Run through the raindrops
    lithely and light.

The little leaves hold you
    as soft as a child,
The little path loves you,
    the path that runs wild.

Who would not love you,
    seeing you move,
Warm-eyed and beautiful
    through the green grove?

Let the rain kiss you,
    trickle through your hair,
Laugh if my fingers mingle
    with it there,

Laugh if my cheek too is
    misty and drips—
Wetness is tender—
    laughter on my lips

The happy, sweet laughter
    of love without pain,
Young love, the strong love,
    burning in the rain.

SONNET

ELIZABETH BARRETT BROWNING

First time he kissed me, he but only kiss'd
The fingers of this hand wherewith I write;
And ever since, it grew more clean and white,
Slow to world-greetings, quick with its "Oh, list,"
When the angels speak. A ring of amethyst
I could not wear here, plainer to my sight,
Than that first kiss. The second pass'd in height
The first, and sought the forehead, and half miss'd,
Half falling on the hair. Oh, beyond meed!
That was the chrism of love, which love's own crown,
With sanctifying sweetness, did precede.
The third upon my lips was folded down
In perfect, purple state; since when, indeed,
I have been proud, and said, "My love, my own!"

THE FIRST DAY

CHRISTINA G. ROSSETTI

I wish I could remember the first day,
First hour, first moment of your meeting me,
If bright or dim the season, it might be
Summer or winter for aught I can say;
So unrecorded did it slip away,
So blind was I to see and to foresee,
So dull to mark the budding of my tree
That would not blossom yet for many a May.
If only I could recollect it, such
A day of days! I let it come and go
As traceless as a thaw of bygone snow;
It seemed to mean so little, meant so much;
If only now I could recall that touch,
First touch of hand in hand—
      Did one but know!

Let the rain kiss you . . .

LOVE ME LITTLE, LOVE ME LONG
AUTHOR UNKNOWN

Love me little, love me long,
Is the burden of my song:
Love that is too hot and strong
Burneth soon to waste.
I am with little well content,
And a little from thee sent
Is enough, with true intent,
To be steadfast friend.
Love me little, love me long,
Is the burden of my song.

Say thou lov'st me while thou live,
I to thee my love will give,
Never dreaming to deceive
While that life endures:
Nay, and after death in sooth,
I to thee will keep my truth,
As now when in my May of youth,
This my love assures.
Love me little, love me long,
Is the burden of my song.

Constant love is moderate ever,
And it will through life persevere,
Give to me that with true endeavor.
I will it restore:
A suit of durance let it be,
For all weathers, that for me,
For the land or for the sea,
Lasting evermore.
Love me little, love me long,
Is the burden of my song.

Say thou lov'st me . . .

My True Love Hath My Heart

Sir Philip Sidney

My true love hath my heart, and I have his,
By just exchange one to the other given:
I hold his dear, and mine he cannot miss.
There never was a better bargain driven:
My true love hath my heart, and I have his.

His heart in me keeps him and me in one;
My heart in him his thoughts and senses guides:
He loves my heart, for once it was his own;
I cherish his because in me it bides:
My true love hath my heart, and I have his.

At Nightfall

Charles Hanson Towne

I need so much the quiet
    of your love
After the day's loud strife;
I need your calm,
    all other things above,
After the stress of life.

I crave the haven that
    in your dear heart lies,
After all toil is done;
I need the starshine
    of your heavenly eyes,
After the day's great sun.

*He loves
my heart . . .*

Forget Thee?

JOHN MOULTRIE

"Forget thee?" If to dream by night
    and muse on thee by day,
If all the worship deep and wild
    a poet's heart can pay,
If prayers in absence breathed for thee
    to heaven's protecting power,
If winged thoughts that flit to thee—
    a thousand in an hour—
If busy fancy blending thee with
    all my future lot—
If this thou call'st "forgetting,"
    thou, indeed, shalt be forgot!

"Forget thee?" Bid the forest birds
    forget their sweetest tune;
"Forget thee?" Bid the sea forget to swell
    beneath the moon;
Bid the thirsty flowers forget to drink
    the eve's refreshing dew;
Thyself forget thine own "dear land,"
    and its "mountains wild and blue."
Forget each old familiar face,
    each long-remember'd spot—
When these things are forgot by thee,
    then thou shalt be forgot!

Keep, if thou wilt, thy maiden peace,
    still calm and fancy-free,
For God forbid thy gladsome heart
    should grow less glad for me;
Yet, while that heart is still unwon,
    oh! bid not mine to rove,
But let it nurse its humble faith
    and uncomplaining love;
If these, preserved for patient years,
    at last avail me not,
Forget me then; but ne'er believe
    that thou canst be forgot!

Answer to a Child's Question

SAMUEL TAYLOR COLERIDGE

Do you ask what the birds say?
    The sparrow, the dove,
The linnet and thrush say,
    "I love and I love!"
In the winter they're silent—
    the wind is so strong;
What it says, I don't know,
    but it sings a loud song.
But green leaves, and blossoms,
    and sunny warm weather,
And singing, and loving—
    all come back together.
But the lark is so brimful
    of gladness and love,
The green fields below him,
    the blue sky above,
That he sings, and he sings;
    and forever sings he—
"I love my love, and my
    love loves me!"

All Paths Lead to You

BLANCHE SHOEMAKER WAGSTAFF

All paths lead to you
Where e'er I stray;
You are the evening star
At the end of day.

All paths lead to you,
Hilltop or low;
You are the white birch
In the sun's glow.

All paths lead to you
Where'er I roam.
You are the lark song
Calling me home!

WE MET ON ROADS OF LAUGHTER

CHARLES DIVINE

We met on roads of laughter,
Both careless at the start,
But other roads came after
And wound around my heart.

There are roads a wise man misses,
And roads where fools will try
To say farewell with kisses,
Touch love and say goodbye.

We met on roads of laughter;
Now wistful roads depart,
For I must hurry after
To overtake my heart.

CONSTANT

EMILY DICKINSON

Alter? When the hills do.
Falter? When the sun
Question if his glory
Be the perfect one.

Surfeit? When the daffodil
Doth of the dew:
Even as herself, O friend!
I will of you!

We met on roads of laughter.

If You But Knew

Author Unknown

If you but knew
How all my days seemed filled
   with dreams of you,
How sometimes in the silent night
Your eyes thrill through me with
   their tender light,
How oft I hear your voice
   when others speak,
How you 'mid other forms I seek,
Oh, love more real than though
   such dreams were true
If you but knew.

Could you but guess
How you alone make all my
   happiness,
How I am more than willing
   for your sake
To stand alone, give all and
   nothing take,
Nor chafe to think you bound
   while I am free,
Quite free, till death, to
   love you silently,
Could you but guess.

Could you but learn
How when you doubt my truth
   I sadly yearn
To tell you all, to stand for
   one brief space
Unfettered, soul to soul,
   as face to face,
To crown you king, my king,
   till life shall end,
My lover and likewise
   my truest friend,
Would you love me, dearest,
   as fondly in return,
Could you but learn?

WILL YOU LOVE ME WHEN I'M OLD?

Author Unknown

I would ask of you, my darling,
A question soft and low,
That gives me many a heartache
As the moments come and go.

Your love I know is truthful,
But the truest love grows cold;
It is this that I would ask you:
Will you love me when I'm old?

Life's morn will soon be waning,
And its evening bells be tolled,
But my heart shall know no sadness
If you'll love me when I'm old.

Down the stream of life together
We are sailing side by side,
Hoping some bright day to anchor
Safe beyond the surging tide.

Today our sky is cloudless,
But the night may clouds unfold;
But, though storms may gather round us,
Will you love me when I'm old?

When my hair shall shade the snowdrift,
And mine eyes shall dimmer grow,
I would lean upon some loved one,
Through the valley as I go.
I would claim of you a promise,

Worth to me a world of gold;
It is only this, my darling,
That you'll love me when I'm old.

MISS YOU

David Cory

Miss you, miss you, miss you;
Everything I do
Echoes with the laughter
And the voice of you.
You're on every corner,
Every turn and twist,
Every old familiar spot
Whispers how you're missed.

Miss you, miss you, miss you.
Everywhere I go
There are poignant memories
Dancing in a row,
Silhouette and shadow
Of your form and face
Substance and reality
Everywhere displace.

Oh, I miss you, miss you!
How I miss you, Girl!
There's a strange, sad silence
'Mid the busy whirl,
Just as tho' the ordinary,
Daily things I do
Wait with me, expectant,
For a word from you.

Miss you, miss you, miss you!
Nothing now seems true,
Only that 'twas heaven
Just to be with you.

Our sky is cloudless.

MYSELF AND ME

GEORGE M. COHAN

I'm the best pal that I ever had;
I like to be with me.
I like to sit and tell myself
Things confidentially.

I often sit and ask me
If I shouldn't or I should,
And I find that my advice to me
Is always pretty good.

I never got acquainted with
Myself till here of late;
And I find myself a bully chum—
I treat me simply great.

I talk with me and walk with me
And show me right and wrong;
I never knew how well myself
And I could get along.

I never try to cheat me;
I'm as truthful as can be;

No matter what may come or go,
I'm on the square with me.

It's great to know yourself and have
A pal that's all your own,
To be such company for yourself—
You're never left alone.

You'll try to dodge the masses,
And you'll find the crowds a joke,
If you only treat yourself as well
As you treat other folk.

I've made a study of myself,
Compared with me the lot,
And I've finally concluded
I'm the best friend I've got.

Just get together with yourself
And trust yourself with you,
And you'll be surprised how well yourself
Will like you if you do.

LOVE ME, SWEET

ELIZABETH BARRETT BROWNING

Love me, sweet, with all thou art,
    Feeling, thinking, seeing—
Love me in the lightest part,
    Love me in full being.

Love me with thine azure eys,
    Made for earnest granting!
Taking color from the skies,
    Can heaven's truth be wanting?

Love me with thine hand stretched out
    Freely—open-minded:
Love me with thy loitering foot,
Hearing one behind it.

Love me with thy voice, that turns
    Sudden faint above me;
Love me with thy blush that burns
    When I murmur "Love me!"

Sally in Our Alley

Henry Carey

Of all the girls that are so smart
There's none like pretty Sally;
She is the darling of my heart,
And she lives in our alley.
There is no lady in the land
Is half so sweet as Sally;
She is the darling of my heart,
And she lives in our alley.

Her father he makes cabbage-nets,
And through the streets does cry 'em;
Her mother she sells laces long
To such as please to buy 'em;
But sure such folks could ne'er beget
So sweet a girl as Sally!
She is the darling of my heart,
And she lives in our alley.

Of all the days that's in the week
I dearly love but one day,
And that's the day that comes betwixt
A Saturday and Monday;

For then I'm dressed all in my best
To walk abroad with Sally;
She is the darling of my heart,
And she lives in our alley.

My master carries me to church,
And often am I blamed
Because I leave him in the lurch
As soon as text is named;
I leave the church in sermon-time
And slink away to Sally;
She is the darling of my heart,
And she lives in our alley.

When Christmas comes about again,
Oh, then I shall have money;
I'll hoard it up, and box it all,
I'll give it to my honey:
I would it were ten thousand pound,
I'd give it all to Sally;
She is the darling of my heart,
And she lives in our alley.

Midsummer

Sydney King Russell

You loved me for a little,
Who could not love me long;
You gave me wings of gladness
And lent my spirit song.

You loved me for an hour
But only with your eyes;
Your lips I could not capture
By storm or by surprise.

Your mouth that I remember
With rush of sudden pain
As one remembers starlight
Or roses after rain . . .

Out of a world of laughter
Suddenly I am sad. . . .
Day and night it haunts me,
The kiss I never had.

FRIENDSHIP

DINAH MARIA MULOCK CRAIK

Oh, the comfort,
    the inexpressible comfort
        of feeling safe with a person,
Having neither to weigh thoughts,
Nor measure words, but pouring them
All right out, just as they are,

Chaff and grain together,
Certain that a faithful hand will
Take and sift them,
Keep what is worth keeping—
And with the breath of kindness
Blow the rest away.

JENNY KISSED ME

Leigh Hunt

Jenny kissed me when we met,
Jumping from the chair she sat in.
Time, you thief! who love to get
Sweets into your list, put that in.
Say I'm weary, say I'm sad;

Say that health and wealth
   have missed me;
Say I'm growing old,
   but add—
Jenny kissed me!

SPRING NIGHT

SARA TEASDALE

The park is filled with night and fog;
The veils are drawn about the world;
The drowsy lights along the path
Are dim and pearled.

Gold and gleaming, the empty streets;
Gold and gleaming, the misty lake;
The mirrored lights, like sunken swords,
Glimmer and shake.

Oh, is it not enough to be
Here with this beauty over me?
My throat should ache with praise, and I
Should kneel in joy beneath the sky.
O Beauty, are you not enough?
Why am I crying after love,
With youth, a singing voice, and eyes
To take earth's wonder with surprise?
Why have I put off my pride,
Why am I unsatisfied—
I, for whom the pensive night
Binds her cloudy hair with light—
I, for whom all beauty burns
Like incense in a million urns?
O Beauty, are you not enough?
Why am I crying after love?

RUTH TO NAOMI

RUTH 1:16

And Ruth said, Intreat me not to leave thee,
or to return from following after thee:
for whither thou goest, I will go;
and where thou lodgest, I will lodge:
thy people shall be my people,
and thy God my God.

How Do I Love Thee?

ELIZABETH BARRETT BROWNING

How do I love thee? Let me count the ways.
I love thee to the depth and breadth and height
My soul can reach, when feeling out of sight
For the ends of Being and ideal Grace.
I love thee to the level of everyday's
Most quiet need, by sun and candlelight.
I love thee freely, as men strive for Right;
I love thee purely, as they turn from Praise.
I love thee with the passion put to use
In my old griefs, and with my childhood's faith.
I love thee with a love I seemed to lose
With my lost saints; I love thee with the breath,
Smiles, tears, of all my life—and, if God choose,
I shall but love thee better after death.

To Know All Is to Forgive All

NIXON WATERMAN

If I knew you and you knew me—
If both of us could clearly see,
And with an inner sight divine
The meaning of your heart and mine—
I'm sure that we would differ less
And clasp our hands in friendliness;
Our thoughts would pleasantly agree
If I knew you, and you knew me.

If I knew you and you knew me,
As each one knows his own self, we
Could look each other in the face
And see therein a truer grace.
Life has so many hidden woes,
So many thorns for every rose;
The "why" of things our hearts would see,
If I knew you and you knew me.

Shall I Compare Thee to a Summer's Day?

WILLIAM SHAKESPEARE

Shall I compare thee to a summer's day?
Thou art more lovely and more temperate.
Rough winds do shake the darling buds of May,
And summer's lease hath all too short a date:
Sometimes too hot the eye of heaven shines,
And often is his gold complexion dimm'd;
And every fair from fair sometimes declines,
By chance, or nature's changing course untrimmed;
But thy eternal summer shall not fade,
Nor lose possession of that fair thou ow'st,
Nor shall death brag thou wander'st in his shade,
When in eternal lines to time thou grow'st;
So long as men can breathe, or eyes can see,
So long lives this, and this gives life to thee.

THE SEARCH

Thomas Curtis Clark

I sought His love in sun and stars
And where the wild seas roll,
And found it not. As mute I stood,
Fear overwhelmed my soul;
But when I gave to one in need,
I found the Lord of Love indeed.

I sought His love in lore of books,
In charts of science's skill;
They left me orphaned as before—
His love eluded still;
Then in despair I breathed a prayer;
The Lord of Love was standing there!

GOOD NIGHT

S. Weir Mitchell

Good night. Good night.
    Ah, good the night
That wraps thee in its silver light.
Good night. No night is good for me
That does not hold a thought of thee.
    Good night.

Good night. Be every night as sweet
As that which made our love complete,
Till that last night, when death shall be
One brief "Good night," for thee and me.
    Good night.

I sought His love in sun and stars.

BLESSED ARE THEY

WILHELMINA STITCH

Blessed are they who are pleasant to live with—
Blessed are they who sing in the morning;
Whose faces have smiles for their early adorning;
Who come down to breakfast companioned by cheer;
Who don't dwell on troubles or entertain fear;
Whose eyes smile forth bravely; whose lips curve to say:
"Life, I salute you! Good morrow, new day!"
Blessed are they who are pleasant to live with—
Blessed are they who treat one another,
Though merely a sister, a father or brother,
With the very same courtesy they would extend
To a casual acquaintance or dearly loved friend;
Who choose for the telling encouraging things;
Who choke back the bitter, the sharp word that stings;
Who bestow love on others throughout the long day—
Pleasant to live with and blessed are they.

NEED OF LOVING

STRICKLAND GILLILAN

Folk need a lot of loving in the morning;
The day is all before, with cares beset—
The cares we know, and they that give no warning;
For love is God's own antidote for fret.

Folk need a heap of loving at the noontime—
In the battle lull, the moment snatched from strife—
Halfway between the waking and the croon time,
While bickering and worriment are rife.

Folk hunger so for loving at the nighttime,
When wearily they take them home to rest—
At slumber song and turning-out-the-light time—
Of all the times for loving, that's the best.

Folk want a lot of loving every minute—
The sympathy of others and their smile!
Till life's end, from the moment they begin it,
Folks need a lot of loving all the while.

He Who Knows Love

Elsa Barker

He who knows Love becomes Love, and his eyes
Behold Love in the heart of everyone,
Even the loveless: as the light of the sun
Is one with all it touches. He is wise
With undivided wisdom, for he lies
In Wisdom's arms. His wanderings are done,
For he has found the Source whence all things run—
The guerdon of the quest, which satisfies.

He who knows Love becomes Love, and he knows
All beings are himself, twin-born of Love.
Melted in Love's own fire, his spirit flows
Into all earthly forms, below, above;
He is the breath and glamour of the rose,
He is the benediction of the dove.

O My Luve's Like a Red, Red Rose

Robert Burns

O my Luve's like a red, red rose
That's newly sprung in June:
O my Luve's like the melodie
That's sweetly played in tune!

As fair art thou, my bonnie lass,
So deep in luve am I;
And I will luve thee still, my dear,
Till a' the seas gang dry:

Till a' the seas gang dry, my dear,
And the rocks melt wi' the sun;
I will luve thee still, my dear,
While the sands o' life shall run.

And fare thee weel, my only Luve!
And fare thee weel awhile!
And I will come again, my Luve,
Tho' it were ten thousand mile.

LOVE

GEORGE HERBERT

Love bade me welcome,
    yet my soul drew back,
Guilty of dust and sin;
But quick-eyed Love,
    observing me grow slack
From my first entrance in,
Drew nearer to me,
    sweetly questioning
If I lack'd anything.
"A guest," I answer'd,
    "worthy to be here."
Love said, "You shall be he."
"I, the unkind, ungrateful?
    Ah, my dear,
I cannot look on Thee."
Love took my hand and,
    smiling, did reply,
"Who made the eyes but I?"
"Truth, Lord, but I have
    marred them; let my shame
Go where it doth deserve."
"And know you not," says Love,
    "who bore the blame?"
"My dear, then I will serve."
"You must sit down," says Love,
    "and taste My meat."
So I did sit and eat.

O my Love's like a red, red rose.

The Promise

of Faith

God the Artist

Angela Morgan

God, when you thought of a pine tree,
How did you think of a star?
God, when you patterned a birdsong,
Flung on a silver string,
How did you know the ecstasy
That crystal call would bring?
How did you think of a bubbling throat
And a beautifully speckled wing?

God, when you fashioned a raindrop,
How did you think of a stem
Bearing a lovely satin leaf
To hold the tiny gem?
How did you know a million drops
Would deck the morning's hem?

Why did you mate the moonlit night
With the honeysuckle vines?
How did you know Madeira bloom
Distilled ecstatic wines?
How did you weave the velvet dusk
Where tangled perfumes are?
God, when you thought of a pine tree,
How did you think of a star?

Smiles

Author Unknown

Smile a smile. While you smile,
    another smiles,
And soon there're miles
    and miles of smiles,
And life's worthwhile
    if you but smile.

Blind

JOHN KENDRICK BANGS

"Show me your God!" the doubter cries.
I point him to the smiling skies;
I show him all the woodland greens;
I show him peaceful sylvan scenes;
I show him winter snows and frost;
I show him waters tempest-tossed;
I show him hills rock-ribbed and strong;
I bid him hear the thrush's song;
I show him flowers in the close—
The lily, violet, and rose;
I show him rivers, babbling streams;
I show him youthful hopes and dreams;
I show him maids with eager hearts;
I show him toilers in the marts;
I show him stars, the moon, the sun;
I show him deeds of kindness done;
I show him joy; I show him care,
And still he holds his doubting air,
And faithless goes his way, for he
Is blind of soul, and cannot see!

A Bag of Tools

R. L. SHARPE

Isn't it strange that Princes and Kings
And clowns that caper in sawdust rings,
And common folks like you and me,
Are Builders for Eternity?

To each is given a bag of tools,
A shapeless mass, and a book of rules;
And each must make, ere life is flown,
A stumbling block or a stepping stone.

The Immortal and the Mortal

George Barlow

Oh, where the immortal and the mortal meet
    In union than of wind and wave more sweet,
        Meet me, O God—
        Where Thou hast trod
I follow, along the blood-print of Thy feet.

Oh, at the point where God and man are one,
Meet me, Thou God; flame on me like the sun;
        I would be part
        Of Thine own heart,
That by my hands Thy love-deeds may be done:

That by my hands Thy love-truths may be shown
And far lands know me for Thy very own;
        That I may bring
        The dead world spring—
The flowers awake, Lord, at Thy word alone.

Oh, to the point where man and God unite,
Raise me, Thou God; transfuse me with Thy light;
        Where I would go
        Thou, God, dost know;
For Thy sake I will face the starless night.

*For Thy sake
I will face the
starless night.*

HE CAME UNTO HIS OWN,
AND HIS OWN RECEIVED HIM NOT

MARY ELIZABETH COLERIDGE

As Christ the Lord was passing by,
    He came, one night, to a cottage door.
    He came, a poor man, to the poor;
He had no bed whereon to lie.

He asked in vain for a crust of bread,
    Standing there in the frozen blast.
    The door was locked and bolted fast.
"Only a beggar!" the poor man said.

Christ the Lord went further on,
    Until He came to a palace gate.
    There a king was keeping his state,
In every window the candles shone.

The king beheld Him out in the cold.
    He left his guests in the banquet-hall.
    He bade his servants tend them all.
"I wait on a Guest I know of old."

"'Tis only a beggar-man!" they said.
    "Yes," he said, "it is Christ the Lord."
    He spoke to Him a kindly word;
He gave Him wine and he gave Him bread.

Now Christ is Lord of Heaven and Hell,
    And all the words of Christ are true.
    He touched the cottage, and it grew;
He touched the palace, and it fell.

The poor man is become a king.
    Never was man so sad as he.
    Sorrow and Sin on the throne make three,
He has no joy in mortal thing.

But the sun streams in at the cottage door
    That stands where once the palace stood.
    And the workman, toiling to earn his food,
Was never a king before.

My Garden

THOMAS EDWARD BROWN

A garden is a lovesome thing, God wot!
Rose plot,
Fringed pool,
Ferned grot—
The veriest school
Of peace; and yet the fool
Contends that God is not—
Not God! in gardens! when the eve is cool?
Nay, but I have a sign;
'Tis very sure God walks in mine.

Faith

WILLIAM WORDSWORTH

　　　I have seen
A curious child, who dwelt upon a tract
Of inland ground, applying to his ear
The convolutions of a smooth-lipped shell;
To which, in silence hushed, his very soul
Listened intensely; and his countenance soon
Brightened with joy; for from within were heard
Murmurings, whereby the monitor expressed
Mysterious union with its native sea.
Even such a shell the universe itself
Is to the ear of Faith; and there are times,
I doubt not, when to you it doth impart
Authentic tidings of invisible things;
Of ebb and flow, and ever-during power;
And central peace, subsisting at the heart
Of endless agitation.

INSPIRATIONS

WILLIAM JAMES DAWSON

Sometimes, I know not why,
   nor how, nor whence,
 A change comes over me,
   and then the task
 Of common life slips from me.
   Would you ask
What power is this which bids
   the world go hence?
 Who knows? I only feel a
   faint perfume
Steal through the rooms of life;
   a saddened sense
Of something lost; a music
   as of brooks
That babble to the sea;
   pathetic looks
 Of closing eyes that in a
   darkened room
 Once dwelt on mine: I feel the
   general doom
Creep nearer, and with God
   I stand alone.
 O mystic sense of sudden
   quickening!
Hope's lark-song rings, or life's
   deep undertone
 Wails through my heart—
   and then I needs must sing.

A garden is a lovesome thing.

FLOWER IN THE CRANNIED WALL

ALFRED, LORD TENNYSON

Flower in the crannied wall,
I pluck you out of the crannies—
Hold you here, root and all, in my hand,
Little flower—but if I could understand
What you are, root and all, and all in all,
I should know what God and man is.

O NEVER STAR WAS LOST

ROBERT BROWNING

O never star
Was lost; here
We all aspire to heaven
    and there is heaven
Above us.
If I stoop
Into a dark tremendous
    sea of cloud,
It is but for a time;
    I press God's lamp
Close to my breast;
    its splendor soon or late
Will pierce the gloom.
    I shall emerge some day.

We all aspire to heaven.

In Summer Fields

Christina Catherine Fraser-Tytler

Sometimes, as in the summer fields
I walk abroad, there comes to me
So strange a sense of mystery,
My heart stands still, my feet must stay,
I am in such strange company.

I look on high—the vasty deep
Of blue outreaches all my mind;
And yet I think beyond to find
Something more vast—and at my feet
The little bryony is twined.

Clouds sailing as to God go by;
Earth, sun, and stars are rushing on;
And faster than swift time, more strong
Than rushing of the worlds, I feel
A something Is, of name unknown.

And turning suddenly away,
Grown sick and dizzy with the sense
Of power, and mine own impotence,
I see the gentle cattle feed
In dumb unthinking innocence.

The great Unknown above; below,
The cawing rooks, the milking-shed;
God's awful silence overhead;
Below, the muddy pool, the path
The thirsty herds of cattle tread.

Sometimes, as in the summer fields
I walk abroad, there comes to me
So wild a sense of mystery,
My senses reel, my reason fails,
I am in such strange company.

Yet somewhere, dimly, I can feel
The wild confusion dwells in me,
And I, in no strange company,
Am the lost link 'twixt Him and these,
And touch Him through the mystery.

MY NEIGHBOR JIM

AUTHOR UNKNOWN

Everything pleased my neighbor Jim,
    When it rained
    He never complained,
But said wet weather suited him.
"There's never too much rain for me,
And this is something like," said he.

When earth was dry as a powder mill,
    He did not sigh
    Because it was dry,
But said if he could have his will,
'Twould be his supreme delight
To live when the sun shone day and night.

When winter came, with its snow and ice,
    He did not scold
    Because it was cold,
But said, "Now this is real nice!
If ever from home I'm bound to go,
I'll move up North with the Esquimaux!"

A cyclone whirled along its track,
    And did him harm;
    It broke his arm
And stripped the coat from off his back,
And, "I would give another limb
To see such a blow again," said Jim.

And when at last his days were told,
    His body bent,
    And strength all spent,
And Jim was growing weak and old,
"I long have wanted to know," he said,
"How it feels to die!" and Jim was dead!

The angel of death had summoned him
    To heaven or—well
    I cannot tell!
But I know that the climate suited Jim,
And cold or hot, it mattered not,
It was to him the long-sought spot.

THE THOUGHTS OF GOD

FRANCES RIDLEY HAVERGAL

They say there is a hollow, safe and still,
    A point of coolness and repose
Within the centre of a flame, where life
        might dwell
Unharmed and unconsumed, as in a
         luminous shell,
    Which the bright walls of fire enclose
In breachless splendour, barrier that no foes
    Could pass at will.

    There is a point of rest
At the great centre of the cyclone's force,
    A silence at its secret source—
A little child might slumber undistressed,
Without the ruffle of one fairy curl,
In that strange central calm amid the
        mighty whirl.
So in the centre of these thoughts of God,
Cyclones of power, consuming glory-fire,
    As we fall o'erawed
Upon our faces, and are lifted higher
By His great gentleness, and carried nigher
Than unredeemèd angels, till we stand
    Even in the hollow of His hand—
    Nay more! we lean upon His breast—
There, there we find a point of perfect rest
    And glorious safety. There we see
    His thoughts to us-ward, thoughts of peace
That stoop to tenderest love; that still increase
With increase of our need; that never change,
That never fail, or falter, or forget.
    O pity infinite!
    O royal mercy free!
    O gentle climax of the depth and height
Of God's most precious thoughts,
        most wonderful, most strange!
    For I am poor and needy, yet
The Lord Himself, Jehovah,
        thinketh upon me!

Wonder

Thomas Traherne

How like an Angel came I down!
  How bright are all things here!
When first among His works I did appear
  O how their glory me did crown!
The world resembled His Eternity,
  In which my soul did walk;
And every thing that I did see
    Did with me talk.

  The skies in their magnificence,
  The lively, lovely air,
Oh how divine, how soft, how sweet,
    how fair!
  The stars did entertain my sense,
And all the works of God, so bright
    and pure,
  So rich and great did seem,
  As if they ever must endure
    In my esteem.

  A native health and innocence
  Within my bones did grow,
And while my God did all his
    Glories show,
  I felt a vigour in my sense
That was all Spirit. I within did flow
  With seas of life, like wine;
  I nothing in the world did know
    But 'twas divine.

  Harsh ragged objects were concealed,
  Oppressions, tears and cries,
Sins, griefs, complaints, dissensions,
    weeping eyes
  Were hid, and only things revealed
Which heavenly Spirits and the
    Angels prize.
  The state of Innocence
  And bliss, not trades and poverties,
    Did fill my sense.

  The streets were paved with
    golden stones,
  The boys and girls were mine,
Oh how did all their lovely faces shine!
  The sons of men were holy ones,
In joy and beauty they appeared to me,
    And every thing which here I found,
  While like an Angel I did see,
    Adorned the ground.

  Rich diamond and pearl and gold
  In every place was seen;
Rare splendours, yellow, blue, red,
    white and green,
  Mine eyes did everywhere behold.
Great wonders clothed with glory
    did appear,
  Amazement was my bliss,
  That and my wealth was everywhere;
    No joy to this!

  Cursed and devised proprieties,
  With envy, avarice
And fraud, those fiends that spoil
    even Paradise,
  Flew from the splendour of mine eyes,
And so did hedges, ditches, limits, bounds,
  I dreamed not aught of those,
  But wandered over all men's grounds,
    And found repose.

  Proprieties themselves were mine,
  And hedges ornaments;
Walls, boxes, coffers, and their
    rich contents
  Did not divide my joys, but all combine.
Clothes, ribbons, jewels, laces, I esteemed
  My joys by others worn:
  For me they all to wear them seemed
    When I was born.

O World, Thou Choosest Not

George Santayana

O World, thou choosest not the better part!
It is not wisdom to be only wise,
And on the inward vision close the eyes,
But it is wisdom to believe the heart.
Columbus found a world, and had no chart,
Save one that faith deciphered in the skies;
To trust the soul's invincible surmise
Was all his science and his only art.
Our knowledge is a torch of smoky pine
That lights the pathway but one step ahead
Across a void of mystery and dread.
Bid, then, the tender light of faith to shine
By which alone the mortal heart is led
Unto the thinking of the thought divine.

The Rhodora: On Being Asked Whence Is the Flower

Ralph Waldo Emerson

In May, when sea-winds pierced our solitudes,
I found the fresh Rhodora in the woods,
Spreading its leafless blooms in a damp nook,
To please the desert and the sluggish brook.
The purple petals, fallen in the pool,
Made the black water with their beauty gay;
Here might the redbird come his plumes to cool,
And court the flower that cheapens his array.
Rhodora! if the sages ask thee why
This charm is wasted on the earth and sky,
Tell them, dear, that if eyes were made for seeing,
Then Beauty is its own excuse for being:
Why thou wert there, O rival of the rose!
I never thought to ask, I never knew:
But, in my simple ignorance, suppose
The self-same Power that brought me
    there brought you.

THE BEATIFIC VISION

Frederick William Orde Ward

Betwixt the dawning and the day it came
    Upon me like a spell,
    While tolled a distant bell,
A wondrous vision but without a name
In pomp of shining mist and shadowed flame,
    Exceeding terrible;
Before me seemed to open awful Space,
    And sheeted tower and spire
    With forms of shrouded 'tire
Arose and beckoned with unearthly grace,
I felt a Presence though I saw no face
    But the dark rolling fire.

And then a Voice as sweet and soft as tears
    But yet of gladness part,
    Thrilled through my inmost heart,
Which told the secret of the solemn years
And swept away the clouds of gloomy fears,
    The riddles raised by art;
Till all my soul was bathed with trembling joy
    And lost in dreadful bliss,
    As at God's very kiss,
While the earth shrivelled up its broken toy,
And like a rose the heavens no longer coy
    Laid bare their blue abyss.

The giant wheels and all the hidden springs
    Of this most beauteous globe,
    Which man may never probe,
Burst on me with a blaze of angel wings
And each bright orb that like a diamond clings
    To the veiled Father's robe:
I saw with vision that was more than sight,
    The levers and the laws
    That fashion stars as straws
And link with perfect loveliness of right,
In the pure duty that is pure delight
    And to one Center draws.

I knew with sudden insight all was best,
    The passion and the pain,
    The searching that seem vain
But lead if by dim blood-stained steps to Rest.
And only are the beatings of God's Breast
    Beneath the iron chain;
I knew each work was blessèd in its place,
    The eagle and the dove,
    While Nature was the glove
Of that dear Hand which everywhere we trace,
I felt a Presence though I saw no face,
    And it was boundless Love.

THE FUTURE

Author Unknown

'Tis well that the future is hid from our sight,
That we walk in the sunshine, nor dream
    of the cloud,
We cherish a flower, think not of the blight,
And dream of the loom that may weave
    us a shroud.

It was good, it was kind in the Wise One above
To fling Destiny's veil o'er the face of our years,

So we see not the blow that shall strike at our love,
And expect not the beam that shall dry up our tears.

Though the cloud may be dark, there is sunshine
    beyond it;
Though the night may be long, yet the morning
    is near;
Though the vale may be deep, there is music around it,
And hope 'mid our sorrow, bright hope is still near.

ON HIS BLINDNESS

JOHN MILTON

When I consider how my light is spent
Ere half my days in this dark world and wide,
And that one talent which is death to hide
Lodged with me useless, though my soul
      more bent
To serve therewith my Maker, and present
My true account, lest he returning chide,
"Doth God exact day-labor, light denied?"
I fondly ask. But Patience, to prevent
That murmur, soon replies, "God doth not need
Either man's work or his own gifts. Who best
Bear his mild yoke, they serve him best.
      His state
Is kingly: thousands at his bidding speed
And post o'er land and ocean without rest;
They also serve who only stand and wait."

LOVE

WILLIAM ALEXANDER

What love I when I love Thee, O my God?
Not corporal beauty, nor the limb of snow,
Nor of loved light the white and pleasant flow,
Nor manna showers, nor streams that flow abroad,
Nor flowers of Heaven, nor small stars of the sod:
Not these, my God, I love, who love Thee so;
Yet love I something better than I know—
A certain light on a more golden road;
A sweetness, not of honey or the hive;
A beauty, not of summer or the spring;
A scent, a music, and a blossoming
Eternal, timeless, placeless, without gyve,
Fair, fadeless, undiminish'd, ever dim—
This, this is what I love in loving Him.

LIE-AWAKE SONG

AMELIA JOSEPHINE BURR

God has a house three streets away,
And every Sunday, rain or shine,
My nurse goes there, her prayers to say.
She's told me of the candles fine
That burning all night long they keep,
Because God never goes to sleep.
Then there's a steeple full of bells:
All through the dark the time it tells.
I like to hear it in the night
And think about those candles bright.
I wonder if God stays awake
For kindness, like the Furnace-man
Who comes before it's day, to make
Our house as pleasant as he can. . . .
I like to watch the sky grow blue,
And think perhaps, the whole
      world through,
No one's awake but just us three—
God, and the Furnace-man, and me.

MAY IT BE MINE

JOHN KENDRICK BANGS

If any round about me play,
And dance and sing in glad array,
And laugh and cheer,
May it be mine to see and hear.

If any toil at noble things,
And strive the higher levellings
To reach and win,
May it be mine to join therein.

IN THE BEGINNING

Angela Morgan

The great God dreamed a dream through me,
Mighty as dream of God could be;
He made me a victorious man,
Shaped me unto a perfect plan,
Summoned me forth to radiant birth
Upon the radiant earth.
He lavished gifts within my hand,
Gave me the power to command
The thundering forces that he hurled
Upon the seething world. . . .
Creation's dream was wondrous good
Had I but understood.
The great God dreamed a dream through me,
But I was blind and could not see.
My royal gifts were laid in rust,
For parentage, I claimed the dust.
Decay and sorrow, age and blight—
These gifts I deemed my right.

The great God spoke a word through me—
That word was *Life*. How can it be
That I, in God's own substance made,
Should face the universe, afraid?
Born of eternal life am I—
Why should I fail and die?
O God, so huge was thine intent,
So greatly was thy passion spent,
This counterpoint is not the plan
That Thou didst dream for man.
'Tis this: Man's dream must mate with thine.
Man's word, man's life, must be divine;
Man must be conscious through and through
To make Thy dream come true!

Born of eternal life am I.

Conquering Fate

Sarah K. Bolton

I like the man who faces what he must
With step triumphant and a heart of cheer;
Who fights the daily battle without fear;
Sees his hopes fail, yet keeps unfaltering trust
That God is God; that somehow, true and just
His plans work out for mortals; not a tear
Is shed when fortune, which the world holds dear,
Falls from his grasp; better, with love, a crust
Than living in dishonor; envies not,
Nor loses faith in man; but does his best
Nor ever mourns over his humbler lot,
But with a smile and words of hope, gives zest
To every toiler; he alone is great,
Who by a life heroic conquers fate.

Up-Hill

Christina G. Rossetti

Does the road wind up-hill all the way?
　　Yes, to the very end.
Will the day's journey take the whole long day?
　　From morn to night, my friend.

But is there for the night a resting place?
　　A roof for when the slow, dark hours begin.
May not the darkness hide it from my face?
　　You cannot miss that inn.

Shall I meet other wayfarers at night?
　　Those who have gone before.
Then must I knock, or call when just in sight?
　　They will not keep you waiting at that door.

Shall I find comfort, travel-sore and weak?
　　Of labor you shall find the sum.
Will there be beds for me and all who seek?
　　Yea, beds for all who come.

LIFE
JOSEPH MORRIS

Life is a seesaw that goes up and down,
Goes up and down, goes up and down;
First it's all sunshine and then it's all frown—
And still it goes up and down.

Life like a pendulum swings to and fro,
Swings to and fro, swings to and fro;
Laughter and teardrops, they come
	and they go—
And still it swings to and fro.

Life is a journey o'er valley and hill,
Valley and hill, valley and hill;
If all were level we'd soon have our fill—
So up and on with a will!

TRY SMILING
AUTHOR UNKNOWN

When the weather suits you not,
	Try smiling;
When your coffe isn't hot,
	Try smiling.
When your neighbors don't do right,
Or your relatives all fight,
Sure 'tis hard, but then you might—
	Try smiling.

Doesn't change the things, of course—
	Just smiling;
But it cannot make them worse,
	Just smiling.
And it seems to help your case,
Brightens up a gloomy place;
Then, it sort o'rests your face—
	Just smiling.

IF I KNEW
AUTHOR UNKNOWN

If I knew the box where the smiles are kept,
No matter how large the key,
Or strong the bolt, I would try so hard,
'Twould open, I know, for me.
Then over the land and sea broadcast,
I'd scatter the smiles to play,
That the children's faces might hold them fast
For many and many a day.

If I knew a box that was large enough
To hold all the frowns I meet,
I would like to gather them, every one,
From nursery, shool, and street;
Then, holding and folding I'd pack them in,
And turning the monster key,
I'd hire a giant to drop the box
Into the depths of the sea.

THE BETTER WAY
LURANA SHELDON

Laugh a little, chaff a little,
	jolly as you go;
Cheer one brother, help another,
	make hope's lantern glow;
Don't be croaking,
	do some joking in a friendly way;
Fun's a winner good as dinner
	for some men, they say.
Scorn self-pity, just be gritty,
	never once cry quits;
Your example may be ample
	to brace other wits.

Then Laugh

Bertha Adams Backus

Build for yourself a strongbox,
Fashion each part with care;
When it's strong as your hand can make it,
Put all your troubles there;
Hide there all thought of your failures
And each bitter cup that you quaff;
Lock all your heartaches within it,
Then sit on the lid and laugh.

Tell no one else its contents,
Never its secrets share;
When you've dropped in your care and worry,
Keep them forever there;
Hide them from sight so completely
That the world will never dream half;
Fasten the strongbox securely—
Then sit on the lid and laugh.

JUST KEEP ON

CLIFTON ABBOTT

Just keep on a-livin' and keep on a-givin',
And keep on a-tryin' to smile;
Just keep on a-singin', a-trustin', and a-clingin'
To the promise of an after while.

For the sun comes up and the sun goes down,
And the morning follows night.
There's a place to rest like a mother's breast,
And a time when things come right.

Just keep on believin' and a-hidin' all your grievin',
And keep on a-tryin' to cheer.
Just keep on a-prayin', a-lovin', and a-sayin'
The things that we love to hear.

For the tide comes in and the tide goes out,
And the dark will all turn bright;
There's a rest from the load and an end to the road,
And a place where things come right.

The Promise

of Hope

Hope's Promise
ESTHER BALDWIN YORK

Hope is
A looking forward to something
With an earnest belief.

Often it means
An expectancy of light
When one is still in darkness.

I like to think of it
As the promise of dawn
To follow the night shadows.

Life takes new strength
And meaning
Where there is hope.

Let us keep this promise
In our hearts.

Hope for Tomorrow
MINNIE KLEMME

Hope thinks tomorrow will be brighter;
Faith knows,
And, knowing, is the surer of the two,
And makes it true.

But when the morrow lengthens into night
And shadows throng,
Hope, like another dawn, transfuses faith
And makes it strong.

Now faith is the substance of things hoped
for, the evidence of things not seen.
HEBREWS 11:1

HOPE

GRACE NOLL CROWELL

This would I hold more precious than fine gold,
This would I keep although all else be lost:
Hope in my heart, that precious, priceless thing,
    hope at any cost.

And God, if its fine luster should be dimmed,
If seemingly through grief it may be spent,
Help me to wait without too much despair—
    too great astonishment.

Let me be patient when my spirit lacks
Its high exuberance, its shining wealth;
Hope is a matter often, God, I know,
    of strength . . . of health.

Help me to wait until the strength returns;
Help me to climb each difficult high slope;
Always within my heart some golden gleam—
    some quenchless spark of hope.

GOD

JAMES COWDEN WALLACE

There is an Eye that never sleeps
Beneath the wing of night;
There is an ear that never shuts
When sink the beams of light.

There is an arm that never tires
When human strength gives way;
There is a love that never fails
When earthly loves decay.

That Eye unseen o'erwatcheth all;
That Arm upholds the sky;
That Ear doth hear the sparrows call;
That Love is ever nigh.

Hope Is a Word

Elma V. Harnetiaux

Hope is a word to live by.
Hope is something within us that makes
    us strive and reach for something higher.
There may be failure, but there is always hope
    to start again, with hope directing our way.

Hope longs for a desired goal.
Hope keeps us with a song in our hearts.
Hope is a booster for the discouraged.

Hope is a stepping stone to the depressed and
    needy; it renews their will to find a
    brighter day.

Hope is confidence and expectation.
Hope is a guide to good cheer and happiness.
Hope is a comfort when fear assails us.
Hope brings light into darkness.
Hope is truly a word to live by.

HOPE IS LIKE THE SUN

PATIENCE STRONG

Hope is like the sun
Upon the threshold of
   the heart.
A glow lights up the
   inner room.
The shadows fall apart,
And rising to unlatch
   the door
We cast all fear away
As we venture out into
The brightness of the day.

Hope is like a ray
   of sunlight
Falling on gray stone.
The heart is warmed.
We're tempted out
To take the road alone,
Out towards a broad horizon
Where the sky is gold
With promise of the
    love of God
And blessings manifold.

GOD KNOWS
AUTHOR UNKNOWN

God knows—not I—the devious way
Wherein my faltering feet may tread
Before, into the light of day,
My steps from out this gloom are led.
And since my Lord the path doth see,
What matter if 'tis hid from me?

God knows—not I—how sweet accord
Shall grow at length from out this clash
Of earthly discords which have jarred
On soul and sense; I hear the crash,
Yet feel and know that on His ear
Breaks harmony—full, deep, and clear.

God knows—not I—why, when I'd fain
Have walked in pastures green and fair,
The path He pointed me hath lain
Through rocky deserts, bleak and bare.
I blindly trust—since 'tis His will—
This way lies safety, that way ill.

He knoweth too, despite my will,
I'm weak when I should be most strong.
And after earnest wrestling still
I see the right yet do the wrong.
Is it that I may learn at length
Not mine but His, the saving strength?

His perfect plan I may not grasp,
Yet I can trust Love Infinite,
And with my feeble fingers clasp
The hand that leads me into light.
My soul upon His errands goes,
The end I know not—but God knows.

Hope is the music of the soul.

Dreams and Realities

PHOEBE CARY

Sometimes, I think, the things we see
Are shadows of the things to be;
That what we plan we build;
That every hope that hath been crossed,
And every dream we thought was lost,
In heaven shall be fulfilled;

And when on that last day we rise,
Caught up between the earth and skies,
Then shall we hear our Lord
Say, Thou hast done with doubt and death,
Henceforth, according to thy faith,
Shall be thy faith's reward.

The Unbroken String

PATIENCE STRONG

Love and friendship, joy and sorrow,
These are the strings on which we play.
These are the notes that go to make
The varied music of the day.

With the passing of the years
The strings of life get frayed and thin—
And youth's high tones are touched
With sadness, like a muted violin.

But there is one undying thing,
One golden string that does not break:
The string of Hope—

We play upon it, and it never fails to wake
An echo in the weary spirit.
One sweet note fresh faith can bring.

For Hope is the music of the soul
Played on the heart's unbroken string.

One Day at a Time
Ralph Waldo Emerson

Finish every day and be done with it.
You have done what you could.
Some blunders and absurdities
    no doubt have crept in;
Forget them as soon as you can.

Tomorrow is a new day;
Begin it well and serenely
And with too high a spirit
    to be cumbered with
Your old nonsense.

This day is all that is
    good and fair.
It is too dear,
With its hopes and invitations,
To waste a moment on the yesterdays.

My Hand in God's
Florence Scripps Kellogg

Each morning when I wake I say,
"I place my hand in God's today."
I know He'll walk close by my side,
My every wandering step to guide.

He leads me with the tenderest care
When paths are dark and I despair.
No need for me to understand,
If I but hold fast to His hand.

My hand in His! No surer way
To walk in safety through each day.
By His great bounty I am fed,
Warmed by His love and comforted.

When at day's end I seek my rest
And realize how much I'm blessed,
My thanks pour out to Him; and then
I place my hand in God's again.

A Happy Day
Author Unknown

A heart full of thankfulness;
A thimbleful of care;
A soul of simple hopefulness;
An early morning prayer;

A smile to greet the morning with;
A kind word as the key

To open the door and greet the day,
Whate'er it brings to thee;

A patient trust in Providence,
To sweeten all the way—
All these, combined with thoughtfulness,
Will make a happy day.

Tomorrow is a new day . . .

HOLD FAST YOUR DREAMS

Louise Driscoll

Hold fast your dreams!
Within your heart
Keep one still, secret spot
Where dreams may go,
And, sheltered so,
May thrive and grow
Where doubt and fear are not.
Oh, keep a place apart,
Within your heart,
For little dreams to go!

Think still of lovely things that
    are not true.
Let wish and magic work at
    will in you.
Be sometimes blind to sorrow.
    Make believe!
Forget the calm that lies
In disillusioned eyes.
Though we all know that
    we must die,
Yet you and I
May walk like gods and be
Even now at home in immortality.

We see so many ugly things—
Deceits and wrongs and quarrelings;
We know, alas! we know
How quickly fade
The color in the west,
The bloom upon the flower,
The bloom upon the breast
And youth's blind hour.
Yet keep within your heart
A place apart
Where little dreams may go,
May thrive and grow.
Hold fast—hold fast your dreams!

A Light in the Window

JOSEPH MORRIS

The evening came, and swiftly fell
The dark of winter's night.
The miles were long; the team, full tired,
Pulled not together quite.
Each turn and bend the horses knew;
We rumbled 'cross the bridge;
The last long hill was reached, and then—
The clearing on the ridge.
The horses broke into a trot;
A light gleamed through the trees;
It beckoned to a glowing hearth
And warmth and food and ease.

When I am outward bound from earth
And past its utmost rim,
I'll grope, no doubt, along weird ways,
'Mid shadows dread and dim;
And as a little child that fears
What is unknown, I'll stray
From realm unto mysterious realm
And often lose my way.
Then through the blackness may there shine
The old familiar light,
And I shall know that I am Home
And come in from the night.

Hope

BEVERLY J. ANDERSON

Hope is a robin
Singing on a rainy day;
He knows the sun will shine again
Though skies may now be gray.

Like the robin let us be,
Meet trouble with a smile;
And the sun will shine for us
In just a little while.

CROSSING THE BAR

Alfred, Lord Tennyson

Sunset and evening star,
And one clear call for me.
And may there be no moaning
    of the bar,
When I put out to sea,

But such a tide as moving seems asleep,
Too full for sound and foam,
When that which drew from out the
    boundless deep
Turns again home.

Twilight and evening bell,
And after that the dark!
And may there be no sadness
    of farewell,
When I embark;

For tho' from out our bourne of
    Time and Place
The flood may bear me far,
I hope to see my Pilot face to face
When I have crossed the bar.

Fear thou not at all . . .

HOPE AND FEAR

ALGERNON CHARLES SWINBURNE

Beneath the shadow of dawn's
   aerial cope,
With eyes enkindled as the
   sun's own sphere,
Hope from the front of youth
   in godlike cheer
Looks Godward, past the shades
   where blind men grope
Round the dark door that prayers
   nor dreams can ope,
And makes for joy the very
   darkness dear
That gives her wide wings play;
   nor dreams that Fear

At noon may rise and pierce
   the heart of Hope.
Then, when the soul leaves off
   to dream and yearn,
May Truth first purge her eyesight
   to discern
What once being known leaves
   time no power to appall;
Till youth at last, ere yet youth
   be not, learn
The kind wise word that falls
   from years that fall—
"Hope not thou much, and fear
   thou not at all."

GREEN GRASS UNDER THE SNOW

ANNIE A. PRESTON

The work of the sun is slow,
But as sure as heaven, we know;
So we'll not forget,
When the skies are wet,
There's green grass under the snow.

When the winds of winter blow,
Wailing like voices of woe,
There are April showers,
And buds and flowers,
And green grass under the snow.

We find that it's ever so,
In this life's uneven flow:
We've only to wait,
In the face of fate,
For the green grass under the snow.

THE LESSON

ARTHUR WALLACE PEACH

Not every day can wear the charm
Of sunbeam's smile and cheery air,
Nor every life know naught of harm,
Or sorrow's cross of care.

But every day that comes with rain
Means brighter sunny days to be;
And every life with hours of pain
Joy's happier hours will see.

This truth the years would have us learn:
By sorrow, joy is sweeter made;
Where fairest roses glow and burn,
The rain's soft lips were laid!

Index